SPECIAL SERMONS
— FOR —
SPECIAL DAYS

To my sisters, Dorothy and Bonnie,
And my brother, Rex.

SPECIAL SERMONS

— FOR —

SPECIAL DAYS

ROGER ELLSWORTH

LOIZEAUX

Neptune, New Jersey

The Scripture quotations in this publication are from
the New King James Version. Copyright 1979, 1980, 1982,
Thomas Nelson, Inc.

Library of Congress Cataloging-in-Publication Data

Ellsworth, Roger, 1948-
Special sermons for special days / Roger Ellsworth.
ISBN 0-87213-150-5 (pbk. : alk. paper)
1. Occasional sermons—Outlines, syllabi, etc.
2. Church year sermons—Outlines, syllabi, etc. I. Title.
BV4254.2.E45 2000
251'.02—dc20   96-24007

Printed in the United States of America
10 9 8 7 6 5 4 3 2 1

CONTENTS

INTRODUCTION

I t was Memorial Day weekend. I decided I would not preach a sermon relating to the occasion, but would stick with my series of expositions of John's gospel. The service no sooner had begun than I was filled with regret. The congregation was larger than usual with many visitors. The special music was geared to the occasion and was received with much appreciation. As I announced that I was continuing my series of sermons from John's gospel, I could detect a disappointment sweep across the congregation. These people had come with Memorial Day on their minds and with the expectation of hearing a Biblical message on that same theme and I had failed them. I determined next year I would preach on a Memorial Day theme.

There are several valid and compelling reasons for the pastor to preach sermons related to the major holidays. Perhaps the major reason is what I've already alluded to, namely the built-in interest factor. The pastor's hearers already have the holiday and its meaning on their minds when they come to church. The truth is many come to the holiday worship service with the expectation of hearing a message that relates to the holiday. If the pastor merely announces, as I did, that he is picking up where he left off last Sunday in his exposition of a particular book, the hearer is disappointed and may even resolve to seek out a more sensible, sensitive preacher in the future.

Preaching holiday themes also gives the pastor part of the answer in dealing with that age-old, tyrannical question: What shall I preach? It is a daunting task to simply select a text or topic for preaching. Some pastors stand before their congregations more than 100 times a year (Sunday mornings, Sunday evenings, and midweek service). How does one provide meaty fare for so many occasions? It is very helpful therefore to have certain texts and themes suggested by the calendar.

Such preaching also provides a nice change of pace for the audiences of the pastor who majors on consecutive exposition of books of the Bible—Genesis in the morning, John in the evening, and Galatians on Wednesday. Even the heartiest members can grow a bit weary with this approach and find themselves yearning for a break.

Perhaps the best reason for preaching holiday themes is simply this: many of the holidays give us the opportunity to preach the great central themes of the Christian faith. This should not be minimized. We live in an age in which there is little understanding of the key doctrines of the Christian faith. The pastor should seize every opportunity therefore to rehearse such themes as Christ's birth, death, and resurrection.

While there are many excellent reasons for preaching on holiday themes, there is also the difficulty of doing such preaching in a fresh and winsome way. Pastors who have a long tenure find holiday preaching to be especially challenging. I am therefore offering a sermon for each of what I consider to be the twelve major occasions of the church year. In each section there is a word of introduction, a bare-bones outline of a message suitable for the occasions, and a fuller outline of the same sermon. The former will give a bird's-eye view of the major thrusts of the sermon while the latter provides some of the major thoughts behind the points.

My hope in compiling these sermons is not only that pastors will be encouraged to preach sermons related to these special days, but that they will also be able to discover some new themes for some of these days, as well as some new thoughts on old themes.

I am grateful to Mr. Peter Bartlett and Loizeaux publishers for their interest and encouragement in developing these sermons. I am also deeply indebted to my wife, Sylvia, and to my secretaries, Susan Bailie and Sheila Ketteman for their assistance.

CHAPTER 1

New Year's Day

The new year is a time of assessment and aspiration, a time of renewal and fresh commitment. It is also a time in which people find themselves wondering what lies ahead and how they will be able to face it.

The truth is the new year will see many in the pastor's congregation walking strange paths, paths they didn't expect to be walking. As they walk these paths they will find themselves asking those familiar *why* questions: why me? why now? And the *how* questions will also press upon them: how do I face this strange situation?

Any sermon that stresses the loving purpose of God for His people and lays out the need to trust Him even when we don't understand will be a source of real encouragement and strength. The Lord's paths may seem strange to us, but they are not to Him. He knows what He wants to achieve in our lives, and He takes us down those paths that will produce the desired result.

The following sermon shows how the Lord led the people of Israel out of Egypt by a strange path, and it also gives some insights into the *whys* and *hows* of that path.

THE LORD LEADING BY STRANGE PATHS

EXODUS 14:1-31

I. The Strangeness of the Path
  A. It Led Them Away from Their Destination
  B. It Led Them into Real Danger
II. The Strategy behind the Path
  A. It Was for the Glory of His Name
  B. It Was for the Good of His People
III. The Strength for the Path
  A. They Were to Trust God's Loving Purpose
  B. They Were to Obey God's Commands

We stand on the brink of a new year. What will it bring to our nation? To our church? To our individual lives? No one can say for sure. One thing we can be sure of is the new year will bring some great challenges to us and probably some great difficulties. We will most assuredly find ourselves traveling paths in the new year that we would never have chosen for ourselves.

How are we to handle the strange paths we often have to tread in life? The experience of the nation of Israel in their departure from Egypt can give us some insight into this vital matter.

I. THE STRANGENESS OF THE PATH

A. *It Led Them Away from Their Destination*

The people of Israel had just been released from their bondage in Egypt so they could return to the land that God had given their father Abraham. Perhaps they thought their troubles were over as they began to make their way out of Succoth. It was, after all, only a short trip up to the land of Canaan.

They hadn't traveled long before they realized they weren't headed for Canaan at all, but were traveling instead in a southeasterly direction. This route would certainly take them out of Egypt, but it would also take them into the wilderness of Sinai, not directly into the land of Canaan.

As they traveled they soon came to the Red Sea. Instead of crossing over it, they traveled parallel to it. They were therefore on the west bank of the Red Sea and still in Egyptian territory. The people must have wondered why they were taking such a strange path. But Moses had led them so skillfully that they were willing to follow him.

B. *It Led Them into Real Danger*

It wasn't long until this strange path got them into terrible danger. While they were journeying along, Pharaoh was having second thoughts about letting them go. Soon he had gathered his army and was in full pursuit. When the people of Israel became aware that Pharaoh was pursuing them, they were hemmed in. The sea was on their east; mountains were on their west; and Pharaoh was behind them.

Their willingness to unquestioningly follow Moses wilted under the pressure of this situation, and they began to murmur and complain (11-12). Why had Moses led them in this strange path?

We certainly have no difficulty identifying with them. We have often found ourselves hemmed in by difficulties and hardships with no way out. The sickness or loss of a loved one; some financial reversal; a friend turning against us; turmoil and tension in the home or on the job—all qualify as strange and difficult paths. In such situations we find ourselves crying out like Israel of old. Why has God let such things happen to us? Why has He led us into such difficult circumstances?

II. THE STRATEGY BEHIND THE PATH

The people of Israel seemed to think it was Moses' obtuseness that caused them to walk this strange path, leading them into such a predicament. But Moses was only following the orders God had given him (1-2). It was God who wanted His people to walk this path. Why? That's the great question. The scriptural record gives us two massive answers to this inquiry.

A. It Was For the Glory of His Name
Twice in this chapter the Lord said He would gain honor or glory over Pharaoh and his army (4,17). Another time He used the phrase "when I have gained honor for Myself" (18).

God is jealous for the honor and glory of His name, and whatever He does is designed to make it apparent that He is God. His acts of judgment show the glory of His justice. His acts of deliverance show the glory of His grace. And all His acts show the glory of His wisdom and His power.

B. It Was for the Good of His People
Scripture explicitly states the Israelites were not yet ready to face the warfare that would be necessary for them to take the land of Canaan (Exodus 13:17). We can say therefore that one purpose God had in leading them this way was to mature them so they could face hardship without wilting.

God also used this experience to cause His people to rely more completely upon Him. They learned there was no help for them other than in the Lord.

Furthermore, through this dilemma God demonstrated the terrible hold sin has on the human heart (evidenced by Pharaoh's pursuit), and the dreadful judgment that finally falls on those who have such hardness of heart.

In verse 31 we are given the results of God using this strange path for His glory and for their good. We read that the Israelites feared God and placed their trust in Him.

The apostle Paul assured us in Romans 8:28 that the twin principles of God's glory and His people's good are still operative in our lives.

III. THE STRENGTH FOR THE PATH

A. *They Were to Trust God's Loving Purpose*

By telling the people to stand still, Moses was urging them to trust God (13). They were to trust Him to reveal what they were to do next.

When we walk strange paths, the first thing we must do is still our hearts in the midst of our circumstances. We do this by reminding ourselves that God, in His loving purpose for us, will not allow anything to come our way that does not promote our good.

B. *They Were to Obey God's Commands*

After standing still in trust until God revealed what they were to do, the people were to go forward (14). This means they were to act in obedience to what God revealed.

CONCLUSION

Whatever strange and challenging paths this new year may require us to walk, we may rest assured that God is at work in them for His glory and our good. We must, like the children of Israel, stand still in trust then move forward in obedience.

CHAPTER 2

Palm Sunday

Palm Sunday provides the pastor with an excellent opportunity to address a subject of vital importance: the tendency to reject Christ as He is, in favor of embracing Christ as we want Him to be.

The crowds that thronged the road into Jerusalem had great enthusiasm and emotion for Christ as long as they thought He was going to do what they wanted done. They wanted Christ to bring the nation of Israel political deliverance from their hated Roman oppressors. When it became apparent that Christ had no such intention, multitudes jumped off His bandwagon fast. Many of those who shouted "Hosanna" on Sunday, no doubt cried "crucify" early on Friday.

Luke's Gospel clearly demonstrates the different agendas at work when Jesus entered Jerusalem. Also in describing Jesus' lament over Jerusalem, Luke gave us the added dimension of pointing out what inevitably comes to those who reject the true Christ.

PALM SUNDAY
AGENDAS AND TRAGEDY

LUKE 19:28-44

I. Two Radically Different Agendas (28-40)
    A. The Agenda of the Multitude
    B. The Agenda of the Messiah
II. The Tragedy of Rejecting Christ's Agenda (41-44)
    A. The Agenda of Jesus Offers Peace to All
    B. The Agenda of Jesus Demands Decision from All
    C. The Agenda of Jesus Culminates in Judgment for
        Many

We often look at things without truly seeing them. If we had been in Jerusalem on that first Palm Sunday morning perhaps we would have been inclined to think all was well. A huge crowd surrounded and hailed Jesus. There was great enthusiasm and emotion. It would seem that Jesus had finally taken His kingdom and the people of Israel finally had their king.

But appearances can be deceiving, and even though it appeared that Jesus and the multitude were on the same page they were actually far apart. Luke's account enables us to see the radically different agendas at work on that day, and it shows us the tragedy that eventually comes to all those who reject Christ's agenda in favor of their own.

I. Two Radically Different Agendas

A. The Agenda of the Multitude

When Jesus and His disciples arrived in the area of Jerusalem for the Passover celebration they found excitement at a fever pitch. The people expected their long awaited Messiah to claim His throne. As far as they were concerned, Jesus was the right man—His recent raising of Lazarus and His other miracles left no doubt in their minds about this. And the Passover was the right time—what better time for deliverance from the Romans than the celebration of the deliverance of their forefathers from Egypt?

Jesus knew the mood of the swarming multitude. He knew they were ready to acclaim Him as their king. All they were waiting for was a definite signal from Him. By issuing regal commands ("go," "find," "bring") and by referring to Himself as "the Lord" (the only time He does so in the gospels) Jesus gave that signal. The disciples and those who happened to overhear what Jesus said to the disciples undoubtedly began to spread the word that Jesus was ready to claim the throne.

As word spread in Bethany about what Jesus was doing, some evidently ran ahead to announce it in Jerusalem. Jesus was then accompanied with one group from Bethany who spread their outer garments before Him, and He was met along the way by another group from Jerusalem. The emotion must have reached a mighty crescendo as these two groups merged into one and cried: "Hosanna!" (Save now!) and "Blessed is the King who comes in the name of the Lord!"

B. The Agenda of the Messiah

1. To Proclaim the True Nature of His Messiahship

The multitude was correct in proclaiming Jesus as their long-awaited Messiah, but they were wrong to think of Him in terms of a political Messiah. If they had read more carefully the Old Testament prophecies they would have understood that their Messiah was to be spiritual in nature, offering deliverance from sin (Isaiah 53). Even the fact that Jesus was riding on a lowly colt indicated that He was not to be regarded as the typical conquering king, but rather as one who was meek and lowly (Zechariah 9:9).

2. To Force the Hand of the Religious Leaders

The religious leaders wanted Jesus dead, but they preferred to wait until the Passover was out of the way so they could do away with Him quietly. But Jesus had a different timetable. He was the Lamb of God who had come to take away sin, therefore it was essential that He be sacrificed on the Passover. By evoking this public display of great enthusiasm, the Lord forced the religious leaders to conclude that something had to be done immediately about Jesus. In concluding this, they were forced to adopt His timetable.

II. THE TRAGEDY OF REJECTING CHRIST'S AGENDA

As Jesus rode along on the colt He came to a point at which the city of Jerusalem and its gleaming magnificent temple could be seen. And there in the midst of that cheering multitude, He burst into tears. A weeping Messiah in the midst of a cheering multitude? What a strange sight!

Why did Jesus weep? Because the city of Jerusalem had been given the opportunity to embrace the spiritual Messiahship the Lord Jesus offered and the peace it promised, but she had spurned the opportunity and rejected the peace. Because of this, devastating judgment lay ahead.

There are powerful, compelling truths for us to consider in the words Jesus spoke about Jerusalem.

A. The Agenda of Jesus Offers Peace to All

Jesus offers, through His atonement, peace with God, which leads us to other types of peace—peace within ourselves and peace with others.

B. The Agenda of Jesus Demands Decision from All

The peace of Christ is now offered freely to all. His offer of peace visits us every time the word of God is preached to us. It visits us every time someone speaks to us about our spiritual condition. How have we responded to these times of visitation when the peace of Christ has been offered to us?

C. The Agenda of Jesus Culminates in Judgment for Many

If we refuse to accept the peace Jesus offers, there is no way remaining for us to ever have peace with God and all the benefits it brings. We have shut ourselves off from our only hope and must now await the just penalty for our sins—eternal destruction.

CONCLUSION

The two agendas at work on that first Palm Sunday are still at work today. We have to choose one or the other. We can either choose to make a Christ of our own liking—a mere human Christ, a Sunday only Christ, or a Christ who has love but not justice. Or we can accept the Christ who alone can make peace between us and God.

CHAPTER 3

Good Friday

The more our society departs from its Christian heritage, the more the pastor has to labor to make the meaning of the various Christian holidays clear. Most people still know that Good Friday commemorates the death of Jesus Christ on a cross, but very few know the meaning of His death. Therefore the pastor must seek to move beyond a mere recounting of the sequence of events on that first Good Friday and explain why these things took place. Having established the meaning of the crucifixion, he will want to go even further and try to convey something of the awesomeness of it all.

Luke's account of the crucifixion provides an excellent launching pad for the pastor as he seeks to bring these two aspects—the meaning and the awesomeness of the cross—to bear upon his congregation.

JESUS' CRUCIFIXION

LUKE 23:33-48

I. The Revelations of the Crucifixion (33-43)
   A. It Revealed the Heart of Jesus (33-34)
      1. A Heart Filled with Faith in God
      2. A Heart Filled with Love for Others
   B. It Revealed the Depth of Man's Sin (35-39)
      1. The Violent Opposition of the Religious Leaders
      2. The Calloused Indifference of the Soldiers
      3. The Mindless Repetition of the Thieves
   C. It Revealed the Way of Salvation (40-43)
      1. An Acknowledgment of Personal Sinfulness
      2. A Confession of Christ's Blamelessness
      3. An Acceptance of Christ's Offer

II. The Results of the Crucifixion (44-49)
   A. Signs and Wonders in Nature (44-46)
      1. A Sign for the Unbelieving World
      2. A Sign for the Religious Establishment
   B. Intense Feelings in Human Hearts (47-48)
      1. The Testimony of the Centurion
      2. The Sorrow of the Multitude

The Old Testament tells us that after a remarkable vision in which he had seen angels ascending and descending a ladder into Heaven Jacob exclaimed: "How awesome is this place!" (Genesis 28:17) Every child of God feels much the same sentiment when he or she comes to any of the gospel accounts of the crucifixion of Jesus. A special sacredness hovers over these pages.

Crucifixion was a common means of execution in Roman times. It wasn't at all unusual for travelers to see crosses silhouetted against the sky. But there was never a crucifixion like the one described in this passage. Jesus was no mere man, and His crucifixion was like no other. It, at one and the same time, testified to great spiritual realities and received testimony from both nature and human hearts.

I. THE REVELATIONS OF THE CRUCIFIXION (33-43)

A. *It Revealed the Heart of Jesus (33-34)*
1. A Heart Filled with Faith in God

The first thing Jesus did on the cross was to call upon His Father. Through the long hours of the night before being crucified Jesus had endured many painful trials. He had been subjected to a sham show of justice, mockery, ridicule, spitting, scourging. A crown of thorns had been brutally jammed on His head; He was paraded and prodded through the streets of Jerusalem. After all this Jesus said, "Father…" Do you see the significance of it all? In the midst of all this, Jesus was still able to call God "Father." He wasn't angry with God or bitter toward Him. His faith in God and love for God were still intact even in the most horrible circumstances.

2. A Heart Filled with Love for Others

We might expect to read that when Jesus cried "Father" He went on to say "help Me!" Instead He showed His great love for sinners by praying for those who were crucifying Him.

Jesus taught in the sermon on the mount that we are to forgive our enemies. He practiced that principle on mount Calvary. To see how fully God answered this prayer one only has to read the book of Acts. There we read of many thousands being saved (Acts 2:31,42; 4:4), and many of these were religious leaders for whom Jesus prayed on this occasion (Acts 6:7).

B. It Revealed the Depth of Man's Sin (35-39)
1. The Violent Opposition of the Religious Leaders (35)
The religious leaders weren't content to merely crucify Jesus. They wanted to gloat over Him. Little did they realize in their gloating that they were in fact proclaiming the truth—Jesus could not save Himself! Their mistake was to think it was weakness that kept Jesus on the cross. Actually it was power—the power of His love for God and others.

2. The Calloused Indifference of the Soldiers (36-37)
William Hendriksen, in his commentary on Luke, wrote: "Poor, poor soldiers! How much did they take home from Calvary? A few pieces of clothing! No truly penitent hearts, no renewed visions, no changed lives, no Savior? Even today, how much—or how little—do some people carry home with them from the church service ...?" (*Luke*, Grand Rapids: Baker Book House, 1978, 1029).

3. The Mindless Repetition of the Thieves (39)
Luke simply wrote that the thieves blasphemed Jesus. Matthew specifically stated that they repeated the things they heard the religious leaders saying (Matthew 27:44). How many today never think about the true meaning of the death of Christ, but merely repeat the misconceptions of others!

C. It Revealed the Way of Salvation (40-43)
1. An Acknowledgment of Personal Sinfulness
The thief acknowledged his worthiness of condemnation.

24

2. A Confession of Christ's Blamelessness
The thief confessed the innocence of Christ.

3. An Acceptance of Christ's Offer
The thief placed his faith in Jesus' ability and willingness to save him.

II. THE RESULTS OF THE CRUCIFIXION (44-49)

A. Signs and Wonders in Nature (44-46)
1. A Sign for the Unbelieving World
The incredible darkness Luke described began at noon, the time of day when it would be most unexpected, and lasted for three hours. It was deep, intense, and unforgettable darkness.

In Scripture darkness often represents judgment. On the cross, Jesus was actually experiencing God's judgment on behalf of sinners. The outer expression of darkness revealed the inner meaning of what was taking place on the cross— Jesus descended into the darkness of Hell for us so we don't have to descend into it ourselves.

2. A Sign for the Religious Establishment (45-46)
The torn veil indicated the passing away of the Old Testament dispensation. There was now no more need for the sacrifices of the Old Testament. They all foreshadowed the death of Christ—the single sacrifice made once for all.

The tearing of this veil took place at three o'clock—the time at which the priests were busy with their duties in the temple. Some have speculated that since this was the Passover, Caiaphas himself may very well have been burning incense before the altar (John 11:49-52).

B. Intense Feelings in Human Hearts (47-48)
1. The Testimony of the Centurion (47)
The death of the Lord Jesus penetrated the calloused

indifference of at least one of the soldiers, and he glorified God by speaking the truth about Jesus.

2. The Sorrow of the Multitude (48)

Many had come to the crucifixion to merely witness a show. They left stricken with the awareness that they had seen something of unusual significance. There can be no doubt that many of those in the crowd on this day were among the three thousand that were saved a few weeks later on the day of Pentecost (Acts 2:41).

CONCLUSION

We have encountered a great number of people as we have walked by the cross again. Which group do you company with? Are you among those who, like the religious leaders, are violently opposed to Jesus? Are you among those who, like the thieves, refuse to think seriously about the cross? Or are you like the forgiven thief and the centurion? Do you understand that it was no ordinary man who died there, but the very Son of God, and that His death there provided salvation for sinners? May God help us to be in this last category.

CHAPTER 4

Easter

Scripture abounds with texts for preaching on the resurrection of Jesus and its implications for His people. The pastor should, of course, diligently study and preach these major texts.

While not neglecting these texts, it is good for the pastor to occasionally seek a fresh perspective. Such a perspective is provided by Luke's account of the conversion of Saul of Tarsus. Here is a man who was supremely convinced that the resurrection of Jesus was a hoax, but to his amazement he learned that it was sober reality. He had been so sure yet so wrong!

Many wander into our churches on Easter Sunday who have much the same mindset Saul had. Hearing a powerful message about one of their own could be the means of bringing them face to face with the risen Lord.

SO SURE AND SO WRONG
A RESURRECTION SKEPTIC
ENCOUNTERS THE LIVING CHRIST

ACTS 9:1-6

I. The Resurrection of Jesus Is an Indisputable Reality (4-5a)
  A. The Evidence Saul Encountered
  B. The Conclusion He Drew
II. Denial of the Resurrection Results in Great Loss (5b)
  A. Saul's Kicking
  B. Saul's Pain
III. Belief in the Resurrection Results in Obedience (6)
  A. Saul's Prayer
  B. The Lord's Response

It was clear to Saul of Tarsus that something had to be done. The disciples of Jesus were filling Jerusalem and the surrounding areas with talk of their master, Jesus, arising from the grave. If the authorities could only produce the body of Jesus, they could shut the mouths of His disciples, but there was no body to be found. Therefore Saul was engaged in the next best thing—persecution of Jesus' followers.

It was this grim business of executing and imprisoning early believers that brought Saul out of Jerusalem and sent him on his way to Damascus. Suddenly he was dazzled by a brilliant light, a light so resplendent that it blinded him and knocked him to the ground. While he was writhing in the dust, he heard a voice saying: "Saul, Saul, why are you persecuting Me?" (4)

Saul learned three truths on the Damascus road that day, truths we would do well to take home to our own hearts on this Easter Sunday.

I. THE RESURRECTION OF JESUS IS AN INDISPUTABLE REALITY (4-5A)

A. *The Evidence Saul Encountered*

After he fell to the ground and heard the voice calling his name, Saul cried: "Who are you Lord?" Imagine his surprise when he heard these words: I am Jesus, whom you are persecuting."

Even though it isn't mentioned in this passage, we know there was more to this experience than Saul simply hearing Jesus speak. He made it clear in later explanations of this experience that he actually saw Jesus in His resurrected body (1 Corinthians 9:1; 15:8). This is a crucial point. The voice could only prove the spirit of Jesus was alive, but it wouldn't necessarily prove His body had come out of the grave.

B. *The Conclusion He Drew*

Imagine what went racing through Saul's mind when he heard those words and saw that form! He must have thought:"It can't be! Not Jesus of Nazareth! He is dead and buried somewhere." But hard on the heels of that thought came the burning question: "If Jesus is dead how can He be here now?"

It hit him at that instant that he had been totally wrong about Jesus. Alexander Maclaren graphically states it:"...the overwhelming conviction was flooded into his soul, that the

Jesus whom he had thought of as a blasphemer, falsely alleged to have risen from the dead, lived in heavenly glory, amid celestial brightness too dazzling for human eyes."

There are many like Saul. They proudly ride along life's road supremely confident that the resurrection is a hoax that has been perpetrated on the human race. Despite all the evidence to the contrary, they insist on believing the body of Jesus is still in that "somewhere" grave where the disciples stashed Him long ago. To all these, we must simply say this: an honest and candid appraisal of the evidence yields only one conclusion, namely, Jesus Christ arose and lives today.

II. DENIAL OF THE RESURRECTION RESULTS IN GREAT LOSS (5B)

A. Saul's Kicking

The living Christ said to the smitten Saul: "It is hard for you to kick against the goads" (NKJV). The Lord's reference was to oxgoads, sharp spikes fastened to the front of oxcarts. If an ox decided to register his unwillingness to pull the cart and kicked at it, those oxgoads would quickly convince him it was more painful to kick than to pull.

B. Saul's Pain

Up to this point, Saul had been mightily kicking against the cart of Christianity, thinking with each kick that he was hurting the church. But he was actually only hurting himself. How did Saul's denial of the resurrection of Jesus hurt him? The answer is it put him at war with the very God he professed to serve.

Time after time, the Bible tells us it was God Himself who raised Jesus from the dead (1 Corinthians 6:14; 15:15; 2 Timothy 1:10). If God raised Jesus from the dead, it is utter folly for a mere mortal to reject Jesus' resurrection. Going to war against God simply cuts us off from all hope for the life to come, and it stores up His wrath until it finally breaks loose with all its fury on the day of judgment. If God has designated Jesus as the bridge from this life into a glorious eternal life, a person is a fool if he burns the bridge or ignores that it is there.

III. Belief in the Resurrection Results in Obedience (6)

A. Saul's Prayer

No sooner had the Lord finished speaking than Saul asked: "Lord what do You want me to do?" (NKJV) His question reveals that he had in the space of a few seconds come to some firm conclusions: If Jesus is risen from the dead, He is Lord. If He is Lord, I am His servant. If I am His servant, I must find out what He wants me to do.

Such simple and profound logic! But amazingly enough there are multitudes who claim to believe in the resurrection of Jesus who have not followed the implications of their belief by living in obedience to the living Lord.

B. The Lord's Response

No sooner had Saul asked his question than he had his answer from the Lord: "Arise and go into the city, and you will be told what you must do." The Lord is eager to have our service, and He will faithfully lead those who will steadfastly follow.

CONCLUSION

The living Lord still intercepts sinners and deals with their hearts. Those with whom He deals have absolutely no doubts about the reality of the living Lord and their responsibility to serve Him.

CHAPTER 5

Mother's Day

The pastor knows most of his congregation will welcome a sermon on the theme of motherhood, but he also yearns to develop that theme in such a way that others in the congregation will feel that the message has deep relevance for them. The Old Testament account of Hannah gives the pastor the opportunity to preach on the theme of motherhood, and at the same time open up themes that will be of interest to all. Hannah dealt with a couple of problems that confront and vex all of us—disappointment and uncertainty. By showing how Hannah dealt with these, the pastor can provide special encouragement to parents, as well as show all his listeners how to deal with these twin perils.

HANNAH: A MODEL
FOR MOTHERS—AND OTHERS

1 SAMUEL 1:1–2:10

I. Facing Life's Disappointments (1:1-18)
  A. Explaining Our Disappointments
  B. Experiencing Our Disappointments
  C. Easing Our Disappointments
II. Facing Life's Uncertainties (1:19–2:10)
  A. God's Present Sufficiency
  B. God's Future Victory

These verses bring before us a godly mother who faced two great crises—personal disappointment and uncertainty. She has great relevance for all Christian parents because we often find ourselves facing the same perils. If we don't know how to deal with these things our effectiveness and our joy as parents will be diminished.

I. FACING LIFE'S DISAPPOINTMENTS (1:1-18)

The first problem Hannah had to face was disappointment over not being able to bear children. Her husband's other wife, Penninah, consistently used this problem to provoke Hannah. Here is the old dilemma. A wicked person appears to be far more blessed than the godly person. Why? Why should the godly person suffer disappointment and heartbreak?

Hannah's experience doesn't give us all the answers to this dilemma, but it demonstrates for us how to live with our *whys* until they are finally dissolved in the glory of God's presence.

A. Explaining our Disappointments

Many leave God out in explaining their disappointments. When a difficulty arises, they explain it be saying God had nothing to do with it. Many see God as the concerned parent in the sky who tries very hard to keep His children out of harm's way, but something always pops up to take Him by surprise.

But a well-meaning, helpless deity is not the explanation for Hannah's disappointment. Scripture flatly says she wasn't able to bear children because "the Lord had closed her womb" (5-6). We may wonder all we want about why God would do such a thing, but the Bible excludes the option of saying God had nothing to do with it. However we may choose to explain our suffering in this life, one thing we can not say is that it takes place without God's knowledge or permission.

B. Experiencing Our Disappointments

Most Christians know God is not a helpless parent who wrings His hands in despair over the trials of His children. But they have not quite been able to master this business of not feeling bitter toward Him about their trials and sufferings. When hardships come they fall into the trap of thinking God has not dealt fairly with them. They become hardened toward God.

All who feel such bitterness lose sight of one thing—God sends trials and disappointments our way because He has nobler purposes in mind than we can possibly comprehend, purposes that always have the best interests of His children at heart (Romans 8:28).

Hannah could have felt bitterness toward God about her disappointment, but she didn't. She had "bitterness of soul" (10), but that only means her childlessness was painful for her, not that she was angry at God about it. If she had been bitter toward God she would never have referred to herself three times as the Lord's "maidservant" (11). What is a maid-servant? It's a woman who exists solely for the purpose of carrying out the desires of her master.

C. Easing Our Disappointments

Hannah didn't know why God had allowed the disappointment of childlessness to come to her, but there were some things she did know. She knew the presence of the trial didn't necessarily mean the permanence of the trial. She knew God had the power to lift it from her. And she knew praying was the means God uses when He employs His power on behalf of His people. She did not give up on God.

II. FACING LIFE'S UNCERTAINTIES (1:19–2:10)

Hannah's prayer was answered and Samuel was born. Hannah was filled with such gratitude to God that she decided to give her son to the service of the Lord (1:27).

How difficult it must have been for Hannah to leave Samuel with Eli! The pain of separation was bad enough, but there was also the pain of uncertainty. These were evil days in Israel. The moral decline had reached even into the very tabernacle of God and tainted the priests (2:12,17,22). In leaving Samuel with Eli, Hannah and her husband seemed to be taking him into the teeth of the storm. How could he turn out to be godly in such circumstances? The wickedness of our own age has caused many Christian parents to ask this same question regarding their children. Hannah's prayer tells us how she handled the uncertainty of those evil times.

A. God's Present Sufficiency

Her prayer contains only a hint or two about the evil circumstances of that day, but it contains a lot about God. Eight times we find her referring to "the Lord." Once we find her using the phrase "the Lord's." Fourteen times we find her using a pronoun for God. That makes a total of twenty-three times that Hannah makes mention of God in a prayer that takes up only ten verses. Her prayer indicates that she occupied herself with the sufficiency of God.

We can say therefore that Hannah glanced at her circumstances, but she gazed at her God. As she gazed upon her God, she saw His power to deliver and preserve His people (2:1-2). She took refuge in the knowledge that He can guard the steps of His people while they walk in a wicked world (9).

B. God's Future Victory

Further we see that Hannah was occupied with God's ultimate victory. She said, "No one is holy like the Lord" (2). Then she continued, "For the Lord is the God of knowledge; And by Him actions are weighed" (3).The former phrase tells us God is not ambivalent or neutral about evil. The latter tells us that no evil escapes His notice. Together they give us rock solid assurance that God has sworn eternal hostility against all evil and He will finally judge it and eliminate it.

CONCLUSION

In handling her disappointment and in coping with uncertainty, Hannah demonstrated some great truths about Christian parenting. The very best thing we can do for our children in these evil days is to trust God fully ourselves and hold before our children His greatness. Great men and great women usually have great parents, and great parents have a great God.

CHAPTER 6

Graduation

Many pastors miss a marvelous opportunity in failing to preach to graduates during the graduation season. It's true, of course, that the number of graduates forms a very small percentage of his total audience, but the wise pastor can construct a sermon that, while directed to the graduates, can be a source of real blessing and inspiration to all.

The following message seeks to clarify priorities for those who have reached this significant stage in life. But since the struggle with priorities is life long, the pastor will find many eager listeners among those who have long since passed the graduation milestone.

TWO GIFTS
FOR GRADUATES

ECCLESIASTES 12:1-7,11,13-14

I. The Gift of Goads
   A. The Purpose of the Goad—to Prod
   B. The Application of the Goad
      1. Don't make pleasure your stopping place
      2. Don't make wealth your stopping place
      3. Don't make work your stopping place
      4. Don't make the accumulation of wisdom your stopping place
      5. Don't make fame and popularity your stopping place
      6. Don't make living for your children your stopping place
II. The Gift of Nails
   A. The Purpose of the Nail—to Fasten
   B. The Driving of the Nail—Give God Priority
      1. What does it mean to give God priority?
      2. Why is it important to give God priority?
      3. When is the time to give God priority?

Each year at this time graduates get lots of congratulations, best wishes, nice gifts, and a ton of advice. The pastor who seeks to add to these feels like he is trying to roller skate in a buffalo herd. But I at least want to make the attempt by offering each of our graduates, not one, but two gifts.

I. THE GIFT OF GOADS

A. *The Purpose of the Goad—to Prod*

We don't hear much about it these days but the goad was a common part of life when Ecclesiastes was written. It was a rod that had one end sharpened to a point. If an ox was pulling a plow or cart and decided to stop in his tracks, his handler would prod him with the goad. The stubborn ox didn't realize when he stopped pulling that he was just lengthening the time until he could get back to the grain and the rest of the barn. He was therefore shortchanging himself. A prod with the goad was a painful reminder to him not to settle down until he was back in the barn.

B. *The Application of the Goad*

We don't like to hear it, but the truth is we are often like stubborn reluctant animals. We always want to stop at some point short of where we are supposed to stop. When we settle down at any point other than the one we should occupy we shortchange ourselves, and we need something to prod and goad us along.

In the book of Ecclesiastes the author, simply known as the Preacher (1:1), applied the goad to us. His purpose was to keep us from settling down in the wrong places. He had himself attempted to settle at certain points along the way and had to endure the sharp points of the goad. Now he applies the goad to anyone who is tempted to repeat his mistake. The Preacher warns us of six potential stopping places that the world has to offer:

1. *Don't make pleasure your stopping place (2:1-3,10)*

2. *Don't make wealth your stopping place (2:4-8; 5:8-17)*

3. *Don't make work your stopping place (2:11)*

4. *Don't make the accumulation of wisdom your stopping place (2:12-16)*

41

5. *Don't make fame and popularity your stopping place (4:13-16)*

6. *Don't make living for your children your stopping place (6:3)*

Isn't it true that most are perfectly willing to settle down with one or two or all of these things as their priorities? Isn't it also true that many who have made these things priorities have found the Preacher's words to be true?

II. THE GIFT OF NAILS

A. The Purpose of the Nail—to Fasten

The gift of goads is to drive us from one point to another until we finally find the place where we ought to be. Once we get there, we need nails to fasten and hold us in place. Some have wandered over the place where they ought to stay many times. They hear about it, rub up against it and then go off to another place. Their problem is they aren't nailed. The nails of life are firm, unshakable convictions that keep us in place.

This is not an age of nails. People change truth as quickly and easily as they change clothes. Recent surveys of American beliefs yield the disturbing conclusion that most Americans no longer believe there is such a thing as absolute truth.

B. The Driving of the Nail—Give God Priority (12:1)

What is it that we need to get nailed down? Where did the Preacher finally stop after trying all the things he wrote about in Ecclesiastes? He settled on God as the true priority or stopping place of his life, and he urged us to do the same thing in these words: "Remember now your Creator" (12:1). By the way, lest we think the Preacher went off the deep end here, the Lord Jesus Christ Himself taught the very same priority: "And you shall love the Lord your God with all your heart, with all your soul, with all your mind, and with all your strength. This is the first commandment" (Mark 12:30).

1. What does it mean to give God priority?

The Preacher gives us the answer to this question in another revealing phrase: "Fear God and keep His commandments (12:13). To give God priority means we hold Him in awe and reverence in our hearts and we practice His commandments. We need to give serious consideration to this phrase. Many say they give God priority, but they have no interest in keeping His commandments. To all these we must say "what God has joined together let no man put asunder."

2. Why is it so important to give God priority?

Why do we need to nail down this business of giving God priority? The answer is God Himself has something nailed down—His judgment seat (Romans 14:10-12). He is going to bring each and everyone of us before His throne to judge us. He is going to see if we have paid attention to the goads that He sent into our lives to prod us away from false priorities or if we stubbornly absorbed their sharp proddings and stayed with our mistaken goals. He is going to check our nails. He is going to determine if we nailed down the true priority of loving and serving Him.

3. When is the time to give God priority?

The Preacher said we should do this in the days of our youth and "before the difficult days come." What are those difficult days? They are the days of advancing age. One would think those would be the days when people would be most concerned about spiritual things. But, sadly, this is not so.

CONCLUSION

May God Himself help each of you to give Him priority

while you are young. And if you are not inclined to do so, may He goad you along until you come to that place where serving Him is the most important thing in life.

CHAPTER 7

Memorial Day

On this occasion the pastor's congregation will be thinking about their departed loved ones. The pastor has therefore the opportunity to be a source of profound comfort and encouragement. But he should also be keenly conscious that many have adopted a "salvation by death" view—all one needs to do to be saved is simply die. He should therefore carefully distinguish between death for the believer and the unbeliever, and plead with those apart from Christ to receive Him.

The following message seems to cover both bases. It does attempt to drink deeply from the well of comfort for those who are believers, while it calls for unbelievers not to assume but to repent and believe.

THE ETERNAL HOPE

1 THESSALONIANS 4:13-18

I. Two Kinds of Sorrow (13)
   A. Sorrowing With Hope
   B. Sorrowing Without Hope
II. Four Blessed Events (15-17)
   A. The Return of the Lord
   B. The Resurrection of the Dead
   C. The Rapture of the Living
   D. The Reunion of the Saints
III. One Solid Foundation (14)
   A. The Purpose of Jesus' Death and Resurrection
   B. The Implication of Jesus' Death and Resurrection

What about our dead loved ones? Will we ever see them again? Or are they lost to us forever? If we do see them, will they be in some sort of nebulous, ghostlike form? Or is there a future for their bodies?

Every serious minded individual has thought about these things at one time or another. Part of living is to think about dying, and it has always been so. Centuries ago the Thessalonian Christians were very troubled over these same questions. They seem to have been riddled with misconceptions about the coming of the Lord. Some may have actually had the impression that only those alive at Jesus' coming would finally be saved. Others may have not gone quite that far, but may have assumed that those who died before the Lord's coming would miss out on the blessings of that event and somehow or another be at a disadvantage. When their loved ones began to pass away and there was no sign of the Lord's return, they were put in a quandary and wrote to Paul for help. What was the future of their dead loved ones? Would they still be included at Jesus' return or were they hopelessly lost?

Paul's words went right to the heart of their troubles by describing for them two kinds of sorrow, four blessed events, and one solid foundation.

I. TWO KINDS OF SORROW (13)

A. Sorrowing With Hope

Paul didn't tell the Thessalonians to not grieve over their dead, but rather not to grieve "as others who have no hope." The Christian is one who can sorrow with hope. He sorrows because he feels the pain of separation, but in the midst of that sorrow he knows he will see his loved one again and that brings him consolation and comfort.

B. Sorrowing Without Hope

The unbeliever, on the other hand, has no such hope to temper and alleviate his sorrow. When he walks away from the grave of his loved one he may hope he will see that person again, but he doesn't have any assurance that he will.

The believer has a fundamentally different view of death than the unbeliever solely because he can look forward to four distinct events detailed by the apostle Paul.

II. FOUR BLESSED EVENTS (15-17)

A. The Return of the Lord

The first event is the return of the Lord from Heaven with a shout, the voice of an archangel, and a blast from the trumpet of God. His people are so precious to Him that He will not send a representative but will Himself come to gather them. This is what the angels emphasized on that day when the disciples stood looking up in the sky after Christ ascended. How empty and disconsolate they must have felt as they saw Him go! But the angels had this reassuring message to share with them: "This same Jesus, who was taken up from you into heaven, will so come in like manner as you saw Him go into heaven" (Acts 1:9-11).

B. The Resurrection of the Dead

With one stroke of his pen, the apostle wiped out all the uncertainty the Thessalonians were feeling about their dead loved ones: "And the dead in Christ will rise first" (16). Now we understand what happens to the Christian when he dies. At the moment a believer dies, his body and soul are separated. The soul immediately goes into the presence of God because, according to Paul, for the believer to be absent from the body is to be present with the Lord (2 Corinthians 5:8).

The body is, of course, placed in the grave. The soul remains in perfect peace with the Lord until Jesus returns. At that time "God will bring with Him those who sleep in Jesus" (14). That means when Jesus comes He will be accompanied by the souls of all those who have died. Their bodies will then be raised from the dead and will be reunited to their souls, and all of this will happen "in a moment, in the twinkling of an eye" (1 Corinthians 15:52) or, if you please, as quick as a flash.

C. The Rapture of the Living

The resurrection of the dead will be followed by the rapture of the living (17). Those Christians who are still alive at the time of the Lord's coming will not have to pass through the bitter experience of death but will be caught up to meet the Lord in the air and will instantaneously be changed. They will receive their glorified resurrection bodies without going through death.

D. The Reunion of the Saints

These astonishing events will be followed by the greatest of all reunions—the reunion of the saints. Imagine it! The saints of all the ages united with each other. Believers reunited. Christian sons and daughters seeing their Christian parents again. Christian husbands and wives seeing each other again. Christians seeing dear Christian friends again. What a day it will be! But as splendid as all these meetings will be, they will pale when the believer meets the Lord Jesus Christ who once before left Heaven's glory to give Himself a ransom for sinners. There in the air those who are caught up will see their Lord and Savior for the very first time. What a moment!

Even the happiest reunions here are tinged with sadness. Reunions here last for a few hours or a few days, and then we have to part from our loved ones again. The best part of this heavenly reunion is we will never be separated again. Paul said: "And thus we shall always be with the Lord" (17).

III. ONE SOLID FOUNDATION (14)

These four events are not the clever inventions of a fertile imagination. Look again at this passage and you will find that Paul based all he said about the future of the believer on this foundation: "Jesus died and rose again."

A. The Implication of Jesus' Death and Resurrection

The Thessalonians had been saved from their sins and had been given eternal life by virtue of Christ's death. None of them would have denied this, but they failed to realize the full implications of it. Jesus died to redeem His people from the ravages of sin. Since physical death is one of the greatest results of sin, Jesus' redemption had to include that or it could not be a complete redemption. If the body of just one believer remains in the grave, Jesus' redemption is not perfect and complete.

The meaning of Jesus' death goes even beyond that. By

paying for our sins, Jesus removed the sin that separated us from God and created a union between Himself and believers. His resurrection therefore guarantees the resurrection of believers. It was Jesus Himself who said: "Because I live, you will live also" (John 14:19).

B. The Appropriation of Jesus' Death and Resurrection

Paul made it clear throughout this passage that the hope he described doesn't apply automatically and indiscriminately to all, but only to those who "believe that Jesus died and rose again" and who are "in Jesus" (14).

There will be a resurrection of the unbeliever also, but it will be one leading only to judgment and eternal destruction. There will be no happy reunion for the unbeliever. Those who want to participate in the glorious future awaiting the people of God must make sure they belong to the people of God by resting themselves totally and unreservedly on the work of the Lord Jesus Christ, not their own work.

CONCLUSION

Paul's words to the Thessalonians pack powerful significance for each one of us. They brim with comfort for believers. We may not only be at peace regarding our fellow believers who have departed this life, but we also may be at peace regarding our own future. We have this peace, not merely because of wishful thinking, but because of the solid foundation we have in the death and resurrection of Christ Jesus.

The same words that comfort the believer, warn and caution the unbeliever. The God who has made all these glorious promises available in Christ tells us we must be in Christ to enjoy them.

CHAPTER 8

Father's Day

Father's Day presents the pastor with one of the most crushing needs of this generation. Families, churches, and society all suffer because men so easily and lightly "check out" in the area of responsibility. Much of this abdication can be traced to men having confused, tangled priorities. And much of it can be traced to men simply not having the courage to stand up for what they know to be right.

One of the ways the pastor can encourage and challenge husbands and fathers to be the men God wants them to be is by going to the classic words in Joshua 24:15: "But as for me and my house, we will serve the Lord." This much used text still speaks powerfully to the needs of the men of this day by addressing the crucial themes of priorities and leadership.

THE GODLY FATHER

JOSHUA 24

I. The Godly Father Knows the Importance of Service
    A. God Demands Our Service
    B. God Deserves Our Service
    C. God Defines Our Service
    D. God Discerns Our Service
II. The Godly Father Knows the Importance of Leadership
    A. Leadership Requires Demonstration
    B. Leadership Requires Determination

More than half of this chapter is taken up with Joshua's farewell address to the people of Israel and their response to it. This address contains one of the best known phrases in the entire Bible: "But as for me and my house, we will serve the Lord" (15). This well-worn phrase contains a world of meaning for every Christian father. It shows us two major trademarks of the godly father.

I. THE GODLY FATHER KNOWS THE IMPORTANCE OF SERVICE

A casual glance at Joshua's message reveals that service to the Lord is the keynote. Some form of the word *serve* is found a total of fourteen times in Joshua's address. The godly father realizes that the priority of his life is summed up in the phrase, "Serve the Lord."

A. God Demands Our Service (2)

Joshua begins his message by saying, "Thus says the Lord God of Israel." He wanted the people to understand that what he was about to say concerning service was not the result of his own observations or speculation. His message on service came to them from God Himself. He was the One demanding their faithful service. Joshua was merely His mouthpiece.

B. God Deserves Our Service (3-13)

Much of Joshua's message is taken up with a rundown of blessings the Lord had bestowed on the people. He is the One who had called their father Abraham out of idolatry (3). He was the One who had delivered them from grinding, oppressive bondage in Egypt (5-7). He was the One who had put up with them and protected them in the wilderness (8-10). He was the One who had driven their enemies out of the land of Canaan and established them in that promised land. (11-13)

God has done no less for those of us who know Him today. We also have been called out of idolatry. We have been delivered from bondage to sin and Satan. We have been the recipients of God's tender care. We have been established in God's own kingdom.

C. God Defines Our Service (14)

In demanding their service, God didn't allow the people of Israel an escape hatch. He clearly defined service so no one could be mistaken about what constitutes true service. True service to God has a negative aspect and a positive aspect. The former involves putting away our idols—all those things which compete with God for our allegiance and our service. The positive aspect consists of fear, sincerity, and truth. Fear means we hold God in reverence and awe and tremble at His displeasure. Sincerity means we serve wholeheartedly. Truth means we serve faithfully.

D. God Discerns Our Service (16-22)

the people seemed to be shocked that Joshua would address them on the matter of serving the Lord. They responded to his plea with these firm words: "Far be it from us that we should forsake the Lord to serve other gods" (16).

All would seem to be well. Joshua had called for service and the people seemed to agree. But Joshua sensed superficiality in their words and warned them of the holiness and jealousy of God (19). If they were not utterly sincere in their commitment to serve, God would detect it and would judge them (20).

II. THE GODLY FATHER KNOWS THE IMPORTANCE OF LEADERSHIP (15)

Joshua was concerned about his nation serving the Lord, but he was also concerned about his own family serving the Lord. In calling the nation to choose whether they would serve the Lord, Joshua announced the choice he had already made for his family: "As for me and my house, we will serve the Lord." In doing this, Joshua was modeling Godly leadership for Christian men of all ages.

A. Leadership Requires Demonstration: "as for me and my house"

Before Joshua announced what his family would do on this matter of serving the Lord, he announced what himself would do ("as for me"). In other words he was committing himself to continue demonstrating a life of service to

God. Husbands and fathers can't expect their wives and children to go where they are not willing to go themselves.

B. Leadership Requires Determination: "We will serve the Lord."

Joshua's words ring with determination. He doesn't simply say, "We want to serve the Lord." It was much stronger than that. It is determination, not desire, that makes us faithful servants of the Lord.

CONCLUSION

Most men in our churches would readily admit that a mighty sweeping spiritual awakening is the paramount need of our nation. Most men know this, and they even desire it. But the thing they don't seem to realize is that such an awakening is not likely to take place apart from individual men getting their priorities straight and leading their families to do the same. A cleansing, refreshing stream of righteousness could be released across this land if men felt this burden and followed Joshua's example.

CHAPTER 9

Independence Day

In our eagerness to apply Scripture to our nation, we often indiscriminately use passages pertaining to Old Testament Israel. The problem is that Israel was in a special covenant relationship with God, and our nation isn't. So while there are applications that can be made to our nation from Israel, the parallel isn't exact.

Daniel 5 however brings before us the truly secular nation of Babylon, and gives us certain clear and legitimate lessons that can be applied with vigor to our own secular nation.

HOW NATIONS COLLAPSE

Daniel 5

I. They Put Gratification above Responsibility (1)
II. They Adopt a Defiant Attitude toward God (2-4,17-24)
III. They Forget a Godly Heritage (10-12)
IV. God Pronounces Sentence (25-31)

There was no greater nation on the face of the earth than Babylon. She had it all—power, prestige, beauty, culture, wealth. But Babylon fell. The somber account is given to us in Daniel 5. While the leaders of Babylon were engaged in drunken debauchery, the Medes and Persians invaded and conquered the city.

Those who had felt the fierce sting of Babylon's power probably thought she was invincible, but she wasn't. Many today think our own beloved nation can't collapse, but she can. How does a nation fall? How does she go from glory to ruin? This passage provides us with some answers.

I. THEY PUT GRATIFICATION ABOVE RESPONSIBILITY (1)

Belshazzar threw his drunken party with full knowledge of the danger. The army of the Medes and Persians had already invaded his domain, and seized all but the city of Babylon. It was a time for vigilance, a time for discipline, a time for responsibility. But Belshazzar chose dissolution and gratification instead.

Our own nation is in a similar situation. Enemies are at the gate. The crime rate spirals. Corruption in government abounds. Lying and cheating are epidemic. Homes are falling apart at a record pace. It is a time of crisis, a time that calls for responsible, disciplined living. But even in such treacherous times, millions still put the emphasis on self-gratification and dissolution.

II. THEY ADOPT A DEFIANT ATTITUDE TOWARD GOD (2-4,17-24)

In the course of the drunken revelry, Belshazzar ordered that the sacred vessels from the temple in Jerusalem be brought to the banquet hall. These vessels had been seized by Nebuchadnezzar in his conquest of Judah and stored in his treasure house (Daniel 1:2).

Nebuchadnezzar conquered many nations, nations which undoubtedly had sacred vessels of their own. But there is no mention of Belshazzar calling for the vessels of any nation except Judah. Why would Belshazzar call specifically for these vessels? He evidently realized that the God Israel was in a category by himself. This is the God who had humbled Nebuchadnezzar (Daniel 4:28-37). This may have caused Belshazzar to harbor a deep hostility toward God, a hostility he chose to express by using this God's sacred vessels for his own pleasure.

The hostility of Belshazzar continues to flourish. Isn't it striking that in a day of many religions only the God of Christianity is attacked and scorned?

III. THEY FORGET A GODLY HERITAGE (10-12)

After Belshazzar's wise men failed to interpret the handwriting on the wall, the queen mother inserted herself into the matter by calling the king's attention to Daniel. Isn't it incredible that Belshazzar had to be informed abut the man who had done so much for Babylon in the past? (Daniel 2:24-49; 4:19-27).

This situation is similar to the one that prevailed centuries before in Egypt. Because of his intimate acquaintance with God, Joseph was used to save the nation from destruction. But a pharaoh arose that knew not Joseph and the descendants of Joseph were enslaved (Exodus 1:8).

One doesn't have to look very hard to determine that Christianity has been to America what Daniel and Joseph were to their respective societies. Christianity had a profound influence on our laws and our institutions. It founded many of our colleges and universities. It built many of our hospitals. But we have come to a time in which many have forgotten or have chosen to ignore these contributions.

IV. GOD PRONOUNCES SENTENCE (25-31)

The words written on Belshazzar's wall constituted God's sentence on him and his kingdom. *Mene* meant Belshazzar's kingdom had reached the number of days God set for it (26). *Tekel* meant Belshazzar himself had been weighed in God's balance and found deficient (27). *Perez* meant Belshazzar's kingdom was to be divided and given to the Medes and Persians (28).

The account closes with the chilling description of the fulfillment of this sentence. The night that began in irresponsibility and dissolution ended with Belshazzar being slain and his kingdom taken by Darius the Mede (30-31). Belshazzar had ignored God until God pronounced his doom, and then it was too late to pay attention to God.

CONCLUSION

Belshazzar stands as a lasting warning to all secular nations. He didn't acknowledge the Lord God of Heaven as his God or as the God of Babylon. He had his own gods, and on this night he was busy praising them (4). But that didn't keep the true God from showing up to write on Belshazzar's wall. And it didn't keep Daniel, the messenger of God, from warning Belshazzar that he was responsible to glorify God (23).

America's well known principle of separation of church and state has been taken by many to mean God must be left completely out of the public domain. Let the word go out clearly and distinctly—America may declare her independence from God, but she is still responsible for His laws and she still falls under His authority.

CHAPTER 10

Labor Day

Although Labor Day is not one of the Christian holidays, it still provides the pastor with a forum for bringing the Christian message to bear upon all of life. The Bible does have, after all, a good bit to say about the Christian view of work.

The following sermon draws from the teachings of the apostle Paul on this matter. It shows how our attitude toward our work can be a decisive element in reaching others for Christ.

By opening the message with the Old Testament account of Hiram putting lilies on top of the pillars he built, the pastor catches the attention of his hearers and paves the way for them to receive the doctrinal teaching of Paul.

LILIES
ON THE PILLARS
— ❧ —

1 Kings 7:22; Ephesians 6:5-8;
Colossians 3:22-24

I. Work from the Heart
  A. The Attitude It Shuns
  B. The Attitudes It Embraces
    1. Fear
    2. Singleness of Heart
    3. Goodwill
II. Work for the Lord
  A. This Makes the Work Delightful
  B. This Makes the Work Powerful

Hiram, who was helping build Solomon's glorious temple, fashioned two pillars of bronze twenty-seven feet tall. Each pillar had a capital that was seven and a half feet tall. Each capital had seven rows of trellis work designs, and two rows of pomegranates. On top of all that Hiram put lily-work.

The fact that Hiram would go to the trouble of putting lily-work where it could barely be seen tells us that he had an attitude toward his work that is rarely seen today. The Scriptures clearly convey that Hiram's attitude should be evident in all of God's children. In his letters to the Ephesians and the Colossians, the apostle Paul even encouraged Christian slaves to put some lilies in their work. Specifically, he urged them to work from the heart and to view their work as work for the Lord.

I. WORK FROM THE HEART

A. The Attitude It Shuns

Paul urged Christian slaves to do their work "not with eyeservice" (Ephesians 6:6; Colossians 3:22). According to Paul, working from the heart is to stop working, so to speak, with the eyes.

Slavery has come to an end in our country, but eyeservice hasn't. To work with eyeservice is to work with one eye on the boss. Eyeservice workers work diligently when he is near and they slack off when he isn't. In other words, they do the bare minimum or just enough to stay out of trouble. They aren't interested in the work at all but only in collecting their wages.

B. The Attitudes It Embraces

1. Fear

The Christian is to do his work, not with a morbid, craven fear as to what will happen to him if he doesn't work, but with a fear of not doing his best. He is to take an interest in the work and not just in himself.

2. Singleness of Heart

This means the Christian is to focus his attention on the matter at hand. He is to give his work undivided attention and effort, and not use his employer's time as though it were his own. The Christian is not even to allow himself to be distracted from his work by the commendable desire to evangelize his co-workers.

3. Goodwill

This means the Christian is to work with the disposition that wishes his employer well. He is not to work with a sour disposition, or in a grudging, resentful sort of way, but happily and conscientiously.

II. WORK FOR THE LORD

Paul stressed this in his letters to the Ephesians and the Colossians. In Ephesians 6 we read three phrases that drive this attitude home: "as to Christ" (5); "as bondservants of Christ, doing the will of God" (6); and "as to the Lord" (7). In other words, he is saying the Christian is to see his work as a way of serving Christ and bringing glory to His name.

A. This Makes the Work Delightful

Work that is monotonous and burdensome becomes a delight when it is seen as work for the Lord. The Christian loves to do things for His Lord. He owes everything to the Lord. By using the word *Christ* (5-6) the apostle was reminding his readers of their salvation. *Christ* means "anointed one," and reminds us that our salvation is all due to the eternal Son of God stepping into human history as the One anointed by God to perform the work of redemption.

What a great work it was! We were enslaved to sin and Satan, without God or hope, and facing eternal destruction; and the Lord Jesus Christ delivered us from all of it. The question we ask ourselves therefore is what we can do for this One who has done all for us. The apostle Paul gives us one answer by telling us we can work gladly and diligently at our jobs. When we realize our daily work is one way we can say thanks to Christ, the drudgery vanishes and delight sets in.

B. This Makes the Work Powerful

Any Christian who tackles his work wholeheartedly as a means of expressing gratitude to God is bound to attract interest. The Bible is full of accounts of Christians who gave their best in every situation, and the powerful impact that attitude had on those around them. When Paul and Silas were in prison, they sang praises to God and had a profound effect on their jailer. Joseph gave his best, even though he had been cruelly treated, and was mightily used of God. It was the same with Daniel and Nehemiah. All served so diligently that they earned the respect of the unbelievers around them.

CONCLUSION

Putting some lily-work into our daily tasks may seem strange and unnecessary, but it is the Christian's obligation. As he fulfills this obligation his work becomes a delight to him and a powerful witness to others.

CHAPTER 11

Thanksgiving Day

Much preaching on the theme of thanksgiving probably seems quite unrealistic to many in our congregations. They know they have been blessed of God in many ways, and they want to be truly thankful. But they are also conscious of bearing substantial burdens. The acute question for many of our hearers is how to balance the reality of blessing with the reality of burden.

Psalm 40 openly deals with both realities, and it helps us see we don't have to be free of burdens in order to be truly thankful for God's gifts.

THE DILEMMA OF THANKSGIVING

PSALM 40:5,11-17

I. The Conflict of Two Realities
   A. God's Innumerable Blessings (5)
   B. Life's Innumerable Burdens (12)
II. The Reconciliation of Two Realities
   A. Praise for the Blessings (16)
   B. Prayer for the Burdens (13, 17)

This Psalm has a twofold significance or application. On one hand, it relates the psalmist's reaction to a particularly harrowing experience. The psalmist described this experience in terms of being delivered from a deep pit of miry clay. He didn't go into detail about the nature of his trouble, but there was no doubt in his mind that his deliverance from that trouble was due to the direct intervention of God. This Psalm is therefore a Psalm of praise and thanksgiving to God.

It is also a messianic Psalm. That means its language and its descriptions can be applied equally well to the experience of Christ Himself. When it is viewed through this lens, the Psalm becomes a conversation between God the Son and God the Father. On the night before He was crucified, the Son indeed found Himself in a great pit of miry clay, but the Father gloriously delivered Him by raising Him from the dead. The Psalm is therefore a prophetic anticipation of the Son glorifying and praising the Father for this deliverance.

In addition to this twofold application, we may say the Psalm has great relevance for the Thanksgiving season. It brings before us the two conflicting realities we are painfully aware of at Thanksgiving, and it gives us some much needed counsel on how to reconcile them.

I. THE CONFLICT OF TWO REALITIES

A. God's Innumerable Blessings (5)

1. His Wonderful Works

The Psalmist said: "Many, O Lord my God, are Your wonderful works Which You have done." Fresh on his mind, of course, was the remarkable deliverance he had experienced, but he didn't limit his thanksgiving to that. Instead he let that experience remind him of all the other blessings God had showered upon him.

2. His Loving Thoughts

As he thought about these many blessings the psalmist realized they all sprang from God thinking about His people. So in addition to thanking God for all His wonderful acts, he continued by praising Him for His loving thoughts:

> And Your thoughts toward us
> Cannot be recounted to You in order;
> If I would declare and speak of them,
> They are more than can be numbered (5).

Thanksgiving Day has, of course, been set aside for the express purpose of thinking of God's blessings. As we contemplate them we certainly have to join the psalmist in saying they are too many to be counted. There are the temporal blessings of family, friends, food, clothing, shelter, healthy bodies and minds, the beauties of nature, and the freedoms we enjoy. On and on the list could go.

But there are also the spiritual blessings we enjoy in and through the Lord Jesus Christ. Was the psalmist delivered from some terrible pit of despondency and depression? Those of us who know God have experienced an even more glorious deliverance—that is, deliverance from the pit of sin and condemnation. And we have been lifted to that high plane on which we enjoy fellowship with God and with our brothers and sisters in Christ.

B. Life's Innumerable Burdens (12)

It's right and good for us to count our blessings, but the fact is there is more to life than blessings. Even though the psalmist rejoiced in God's innumerable blessings, he could not get away from what seemed to be innumerable difficulties. He wrote:

> For innumerable evils have surrounded me;
> My iniquities have overtaken me,
>   so that I am not able to look up;
> They are more than the hairs of my head;
> Therefore my heart fails me (12).

Life wasn't just a stroll in the park for the psalmist. Yes, he had countless blessings, but he also had massive burdens. He referred to "evils" surrounding him—a reference, it would seem, to all the ills created by sinful men and women. In addition to this, the psalmist felt the burden of his own sins, a burden so great he felt he was not even able to look up.

Every child of God can identify with this man in his two-fold burden. We also find ourselves surrounded by an evil society, and we all carry within our hearts a cesspool of iniquity that makes us groan and sigh.

Here then are the two conflicting realities of life—innumerable blessings and innumerable difficulties. These realities raise a sharp, piercing question: How can we be thankful for God's blessings when there is so much evil around?

This dilemma is so sharp many can't stand the tension. Some choose to simply focus on the blessings of life and ignore the evil. Others dwell exclusively on the evils and ignore the blessings. What should our response be? Should we gather around our tables this Thanksgiving and rejoice in our blessings while ignoring the evil? Or should we, in light of all the evil around us, ignore all our blessings and simply refuse to acknowledge God and give thanks?

II. THE RECONCILIATION OF TWO REALITIES

The psalmist gave us some insight on this matter. He said, in effect, that we must not embrace one of these realities while ignoring the other. We must both give God thanks for our blessings and at the same time feel the burden of this evil world and our own evil hearts. How are we to hold these two things in tandem? David tells us we must utilize a combination of praise and prayer in our lives.

A. *Praise for the Blessings (16)*
The element of praise will keep us from becoming so overwhelmed with evil that we are in a continual state of despondency. But it is also in and of itself a mighty weapon for overcoming evil.

How does praise help us overcome evil? It attracts those who don't know God. When they embrace Him as Lord, they begin to live for His honor and glory, and that means they declare war on evil in their lives. As the number of people who know God increases, evil will decrease in our society.

B. *Prayer for the Burdens (13, 17)*
The other half of the combination for victorious living is prayer. The psalmist praised God, but he also prayed for deliverance from the evil in his world and in his own heart. Some of us are more concerned about the Lord delivering us from the evil of others, than we are about being delivered

from the evil in our own hearts. The psalmist asked God to deliver him from both. We have no right to complain abut evil around us until we take dead aim on the evil within us.

God can and does indeed deliver us from the evil in this world in various ways, but the final deliverance comes when He takes us out of this world to be a part of His heavenly kingdom (2 Timothy 4:18). Much of our success in handling the evil here comes from looking forward to that glorious day when we will be forever freed from it.

CONCLUSION

We do not give thanks this year because we have all blessings and no burdens. Rather we give thanks because God's mercy has bestowed innumerable blessings and because ultimately His mercy is greater than our burdens. His mercy is so great that even our burdens can be transformed into blessings. The apostle Paul said, "And we know that all things work together for good to those who love God, to those who are the called according to His purpose" (Romans 8:28).

CHAPTER 12

Christmas

As our society drifts farther and farther away from its Christian heritage, it is more vital than ever for pastors to clearly and winsomely proclaim the true meaning of Christmas. Luke 2 gets a workout this time of year in our churches, but it is still the best text to use in setting forth the message of Christmas and in seeking to convey the awesomeness of that message.

THE MESSAGE OF CHRISTMAS

LUKE 2:8-20

I. The Announcement of the Herald (8-12)
   A. He Reassured the Shepherds (8-10)
   B. He Revealed the Savior (11)
   C. He Reported a Sign (12)
II. The Adoration of the Host (13-14)
   A. An Anthem of Praise to God
   B. An Anthem of Peace to Men
III. The Actions of the Hearers (15-20)
   A. They Sought the Baby (15-16)
   B. They Shared the News (17-19)
   C. They Rejoiced in the Lord (20)

We frequently read accounts of professional athletes wanting to renegotiate their contracts. It doesn't seem to matter that they already have a long-term, lucrative contract. They see their peers getting even better contracts, they conclude they are entitled to the same, and they demand renegotiation.

The renegotiating mentality has crept into the Christmas season. Many want to remove all religious content from Christmas and make a completely secular (and commercial) holiday. The more this mentality evidences itself, the more Christians need to insist that Christmas is not a matter of personal preference and whim. God has defined it once and for all, and the matter is not open for negotiation.

The message of the angels to the shepherds makes clear the true meaning of Christmas. The account of their message fits into three distinct parts.

I. THE ANNOUNCEMENT OF THE HERALD (8-12)

A. *He Reassured the Shepherds (8-10)*

It's easy to see why the shepherds needed this. There they were in the midst of what seemed just another ordinary night when this angel appeared with the glory of God Himself shining all around. This is not the type of thing that makes one yawn and throw another log on the fire. The sight terrified them! So the angel first allayed their fears by telling them he had come to bring "good tidings of great joy."

B. *He Revealed the Savior (11)*

Then the angel proceeded to the core of his announcement: "For there is born to you this day in the city of David a Savior, who is Christ the Lord."

1. *Savior* means "deliverer." Most of the Jews equated deliverance with liberation from the oppressive bondage of Rome. However, the angel who announced the conception of Jesus to Joseph made it explicitly clear that the purpose of Jesus' coming was to deliver people from their sins (Matthew 1:21).

2. *Christ* means "anointed One." It is an official title designating Jesus as the promised Messiah. In the Old Testament the word *anointed* is applied to three offices. Priests were anointed with holy oil (Exodus 40:13-15); Leviticus 16:32). God called the prophets "My anointed ones" (Psalm 105:15). And the king of Israel was called on various occasions "the Lord's anointed" (1 Samuel 24:6).

The life and work of Jesus encompassed all three of these offices. In His preaching, He performed the office of prophet by representing God to men. In His death, He performed the office of priest by representing men before God. He is now at the right hand of the Father to rule and reign over all those who believe.

3. *Lord* means "exalted one." Jesus was anointed of God to be King, but He is Lord over all by virtue of His own person. He is God Himself and therefore has authority over all.

C. He Reported a Sign (12)

So a special baby had been born. But there must have been many babies in Bethlehem that night. How were the shepherds to know the one to which the angel was referring? The angel gave a sign to help the shepherds: "You will find a Babe wrapped in swaddling cloths, lying in a manger."

Our of all the babies in Bethlehem that night, only one would be found in a lowly stable, lying in a manger. How low God stooped to provide redemption! All the way from Heaven's glory to a stable!

II. THE ADORATION OF THE HOST (13-14)

A. An Anthem of Praise to God

The announcement of the angel caused a whole host of angels to burst into this song of adoring praise: "Glory to God in the highest, And on earth peace, goodwill toward men!"

Most are quite ready and willing to embrace the last half of this chorus. Nothing moves them like the thought of peace on this weary, war-torn earth. But start talking about the first part of this strain and they get nervous. They want the peace, but they don't want to bow in submission before God. But Christmas means God has done something. It means He sent the Savior and is therefore worthy of all glory.

B. An Anthem of Peace to Men

Because of what God did in sending Jesus, men and women can have peace with God, peace within themselves, and peace with each other. However, this peace is available only through God's gift of Jesus. The tragedy is that so many want to have the peace the angels sang about without receiving the peace-giver, Jesus.

III. THE ACTION OF THE HEARERS (15-20)

Try to picture yourself being with those shepherds on that night. Suppose you had heard the one angel announce the birth of Jesus and all the other angels burst into praise. What would you have done? You certainly wouldn't have fluffed your pillow, rolled over, and gone to sleep! You would have done the same things those shepherds did. They went to see the baby (15-16), they shared the good news about the baby (17-18), and they praised and glorified God for all they had seen and heard (20).

We should be doing those very things now. We should seek the Savior, and not rest until we have found Him and made Him our Lord and Savior. We should then tell others about the Savior we have found. And we should constantly praise the God of Heaven for sending a Savior to such a sinful world.

CONCLUSION

This is, as the saying goes, "what it's all about." The meaning of Christmas is settled. It isn't our place to debate and dispute it, but by the grace of God to receive it and rejoice in it.